# WINTER

A collection of
Poems, Songs and Stories
for young children

**Wynstones
Press**

Published by
Wynstones Press
Stourbridge
England.
Email: info@wynstonespress.com
Website: www.wynstonespress.com

First Published 1978 by Wynstones Press
Second edition with music 1983
Fully revised third edition 1999.  Reprinted 2005, 2010, 2015.

Editors: Jennifer Aulie and Margret Meyerkort

Cover illustration of 'The Cobbler' by David Newbatt

Typeset by Wynstones Press.
Printed in EU.

British Library CIP data available.

ISBN 9780 946206 490

# Winter

This is one in a series of 6 books:
Spring, Summer, Autumn, Winter, Spindrift and Gateways.

The four seasonal books comprise a wide selection of poems, songs and stories appropriate to the time of year, including much material for the celebration of festivals.

Spindrift contains verses and songs describing the world of daily work and practical life, together with a selection of stories from around the world.

Gateways comprises verses and songs for the Morning time, the Evening time and to accompany a variety of traditional Fairytales, together with poems, songs and stories for the celebration of Birthdays.

*Warmest thanks* to all who have contributed to and supported this work: parents, teachers and friends from Steiner Waldorf Schools in Australia, Britain, Canada, Eire, Estonia, New Zealand, Norway, South Africa and the United States. Grateful thanks also to publishers who have permitted the use of copyright material, acknowledgements for which are at the end of the volume.

# INDEX

*Indexes of first lines*

## POEMS

5

## SONGS

*Index of titles*
**STORIES**

# The Value of Music in the Life of the Young Child

*Free Play in a Waldorf Kindergarten.* It is a winter morning: the twenty children are busy with their work. The youngest, three- and four-year-olds, are helping the teacher chop apples for snack; some five-year-old girls are taking care of their "children" in the doll corner; next to them are a group of five-year-old boys and girls who are sitting at a round table polishing stones, grating chestnuts and chatting together. In the centre of the room an observant and energetic four-year-old boy is directing the six-year-olds in the construction of a snowplough: tables are stacked on each other, chairs turned upside down and leaned against the tables for the front part of the plough. A large basket of chestnuts is balanced on top of the plough. The chestnuts are grit and salt, to be scattered later on the ploughed streets. The room is small and the noise level is moderately high.

Underneath the windows, on the carpet where the children have a free space to build up scenes and play with standing puppets and animals, a six-year-old girl sits, absorbed in her work. She has laid out a forest of pine cones, which stands on the banks of a river of blue cloth. Stepping stones allow the poor shepherd boy, who lives at the edge of the forest, to cross the river and wind his way to the castle gates nearby . . . The princess, leaning out of her tower, sees him coming and calls down to him . . .

As she lays out the scene, the girl accompanies her actions with narrative, speaking in a soft tone, sometimes almost whispering to herself. When the puppets begin to live in the scene her voice changes, becoming more sung than spoken, the pitch of her spoken voice being taken over by her singing voice. Her recitative is not sing-song rhythmic, but the rhythm freely moves with the intention of the shepherd boy as he jumps from stone to stone. The pitch of the girl's voice is a colourful monotone: the pitch remains much the same, but the tone colour is enlivened through the intensity and quality of the words as the shepherd crosses the stream. There are moments when a word is spoken, then the narrative is sung again.

When the shepherd arrives at the castle gates, the princess calls down to him from her high tower. She is far away, and the girl reaches up with her voice to the distant place where the princess lives, and sings her greetings down to the shepherd. The girl's voice is high now, but the intervals she sings are not large, they are between a third and a fifth. The high pitch of her voice, although it is not loud, has attracted some of the five-year-olds: several come over to the rug and lie on their stomachs, watching the play unfold. The shepherd now tells the princess of his wish that she come down and go with him. The simple recitative changes to a declamatory aria: a melody of several different tones arises, moving stepwise, the girl's voice becomes more intense as the shepherd pleads his cause. There is little repetition in the melody, but the movement contained in it provides a musical mood which waits expectantly for the princess's reply . . .

In the meantime, the snowplough has already cleared quite a few streets. It has come back to make a second round to scatter the grit and salt . . . The four-year-olds slicing apples jump up from the table. The noise of all those chestnuts hitting a wooden floor is so wonderful, they want to join the fun! The "mothers" putting their children to bed are angry that the snowplough has woken up their little ones, now the babies are crying . . . Some of the children polishing stones and grating chestnuts try throwing their stones and chestnuts on the floor – what a good idea, it makes a lovely *cracking* sound . . .

. . . the five-year-olds listening to the play hold their breaths as the princess agrees to go with the shepherd but he must first ask permission from her father, the king . . . The princess's instructions are sung to him in a melody of seconds with a strong, definite rhythm . . .

An observer can hardly believe that the chestnut-strewn chaos in the other half of the room (which the teacher is quickly helping to put right again) does not seem to penetrate the sheath of peacefulness which surrounds the puppet play. The children gathered around it show no sign that anything else in the room has taken place . . .

At the successful conclusion of the play, the children watching it lie still. The girl covers the scene with a cloth and sings in a half-whispering tone a farewell to the story of the shepherd and the princess. As her voice fades, there is a moment of absolute silence. Then the five-year-olds run back to the polishing table and the girl goes to the teacher to ask how long it will be until snack.

This description of a six-year-old girl's singing contains many elements of what has come to be called "Mood of the Fifth" music: the singing follows the rhythm of speech; melodies are simple, moving within intervals of seconds and thirds – sometimes as large as a fifth, rarely larger; melodies are often sung on one tone, the pitch taken from the speaking voice; the melodies are not written in major or in minor keys and have an open-ended feel to them. Above all is the mood of the music: when sung properly it seems to reach out and enfold the children in a protective sheath which has a quality of stillness and peace, although the children themselves may be active within it.

This music is a musical expression of an experience which is striven for in all aspects of Waldorf Education. It is difficult to describe in words, perhaps: "I am centred in my activity," "My thinking, feeling and willing are in balance." One feels deeply united with a task, at peace and yet still active. The young child finds this mood in play. S/he is deeply engaged in an activity which is then no longer interesting when the activity is over. The moment of silence at the end of the play was not a moment of reflection, but a moment which allowed the activity of watching the play to come to a complete end before the next task could engage the children's attention.

The broader context of this musical experience should be noted: the kindergarten just described is one where mood-of-the-fifth music was not cultivated by the teacher. The children learned only traditional children's songs and games which were sung in strict rhythm, and with major or minor key melodies. The six-year-old girl experienced similar music at home.

Yet the girl's singing is not an isolated or unusual musical event. Such singing can often be heard when a child's attention is fully engaged in his/her play. We grown-ups tend to dismiss such fragments of melody as noise, or incomplete attempts by the child to sing our music, not listening closely enough to discover the innate coherence of the child's activity. Too often well-meaning adults try to "correct" the pitch which is too high, or the rhythm which is irregular, and slowly wall in a living musicality with "proper" songs . . . Sooner or later, often at puberty, an attempt is made at breaking through these walls, as the pounding beat of popular music has long suggested.

The use of "Mood of the Fifth" music in the kindergarten encompasses two considerations. It is first of all a path of musical development for the adult, which schools his/her musical perception and ability so that s/he is able to participate in a musicality which the children *already possess*. This musicality may, for many reasons, lie dormant or misshapen within an individual child or group of children. Through the adult's use of Mood of the Fifth s/he can reawaken and bring back into movement the musicality which is so essential for the full development of the child's soul life. (To be labelled "unmusical" or "tone deaf" causes deep, lingering wounds to the child's self esteem. There are unfortunately many adults who can attest to the truth of this statement out of their own experience.)

Mood of the Fifth music can also help the adult to establish an additional point of contact with the child which shows him/her that the adult *understands.* One of the rewards of working with young children is surely the open look of delight on a child's face when s/he hears a story, plays a game, experiences something which pleases him/her. The look of delight means more, however, than just "I like that." On a deeper level it expresses the child's trust in the adult: "You know who I am, and what you offer me is that which I am searching for with my deepest intentions. I can follow you."

The present day task of the Waldorf Kindergarten is primarily a therapeutic one. It provides children with basic experiences which they need for healthy development, overcoming deficiencies which often occur today in the first years of life. A very large part of these experiences are sensory, as the development of the physical senses (touch, balance, etc.) lays the foundation for the later unfolding of the spiritual capacities (thinking, speech, etc.). The kindergarten is not a mirror of our daily lives, but an extract of the many activities, distilled to their essence. This provides a simplicity and basic necessity for the content of kindergarten life which the child can understand and imitate wholeheartedly. The meaningful activity around the child awakens his/her interest in the world, and this interest becomes the mainspring of later learning.

In the arts the materials presented to the child are restricted to essentials, and with these the child's imagination has free rein. This can be clearly seen, for example, in painting: the three primary colours are used – red, yellow and blue. The children are given watercolours, a large wet sheet of paper and a broad brush to paint with. The materials themselves preclude any precise drawing, colours flow into one another, sometimes mixing, sometimes remaining pure side by side. There is no right or wrong way of using the colours, the expansive, fiery or cool moods of the colours themselves guide the child's brush. The medium of water enables the child's soul to breathe freely in the movement of colour with the brush. If only the paper were bigger s/he could paint on and on . . .

Music can be approached in a similar way. Here as well the materials can be restricted so that the *activity* becomes of foremost importance. Only five different tones of our twelve tone system are used:

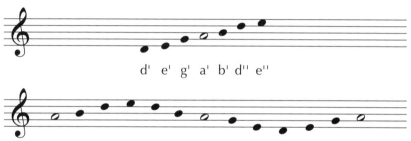

d' e' g' a' b' d'' e''

When a children's harp or lyre is used, the strings are tuned to pure fifths (like a violin's open strings) rather than the tempered intervals of the piano. The songs are not written in major or minor keys, but tend to circle around the middle tone, a'. The rhythm is free, either gently swinging (3 or 6 beats) or walking (2 or 4 beats), but the movement of the music takes its impulse from the words and seeks to accompany its inner content.

This style of music making lends itself wonderfully to the activities of circle time where movement, the spoken word and song freely flow from one to the other, just as the three basic colours do in painting. Teachers who have worked with Mood of the Fifth music in the classroom also know of its effectiveness in creating moments where the attention of all of the children is engaged, enabling a special mood to arise, whether in a puppet play, grace before meal, etc.

Newcomers to this music may at first experience difficulty in hearing the melodies or finding an inner connection to them. Others may have trouble finding the beginning pitch or singing the songs as high as they are written. None of these difficulties should be considered unsolvable problems.

Over time, the practice of Music of the Fifth songs often leads to a good sense of pitch. The voice gradually learns the placement of the tones, and the reduced number of tones make sight-singing possible even for the "unmusical" person.

Difficulty in reaching the higher notes ( d", e" ), which lie within traditional singing range of soprano and altos, can be due to breathing which is too shallow, as well as to the false idea that high notes are more difficult to sing and require greater effort. In the long run, the question of extending the vocal range is best addressed by an experienced teacher. But those without a teacher can still consider the following: the vocal range can be affected by physical movement. Often much can be accomplished by accompanying a song with large, simple, physical gestures. This helps free the breathing, allowing greater ease in reaching notes which are "too high." The songs can be practised with movement until the feeling of vocal mobility is secure. Then the outward movement can gradually become smaller and disappear altogether, all the while maintaining the inner freedom of movement in the voice.

An essential guide for adults who wish to find a path into the experience of Mood of the Fifth music can be found in Julius Knierim's *Songs in the Mood of the Fifth (Quintenlieder)*. This succinct and clearly written booklet describes, with simple exercises and musical examples, a path which really can be taken by all who have a sincere interest in further development of their musical abilities. By working with the suggestions contained in Julius Knierim's essay, the serious student can develop capacities which not only lead him/her into the musical world of the young child, but can help build a new relationship to traditional classical music, and to all further musical development.

Rudolf Steiner, in discussing music for the young child, spoke of the great importance of the Quintenstimmung = *Mood* of the Fifth. The suggestions mentioned in this article, and most especially in Dr. Knierim's book, are guideposts by which adults may find the way into this mood. They are not the mood itself. Individual observation, experimentation, and practice are the means by which the letter of the law may be enlivened by its spirit.

The goal of these booklets is to offer immediate practical help in working with young children. It is for this reason that a variety of musical styles is included. All songs (as well as stories and verses) have proved their worth in Waldorf kindergartens or other settings with young children. Some traditional tunes with new words have been included, and many traditional rhymes have been set to new melodies (either pentatonic or Mood of the Fifth). Familiar children's songs have been excluded for the most part because these are readily available in other collections. Most songs are set in D-pentatonic. This is done for pedagogical as well as practical reasons (see references). Experience has shown that many teachers and parents who wish to consciously address music-making with the young child are often just those who are themselves struggling with their own musical education. With most songs written in D-pentatonic mode (which are tones of a Choroi flute or children's harp, and are easy to play on a traditional recorder), it is hoped that the initial difficulties with note reading and transposition will be eased. The use of bar lines and time signatures varies, showing new possibilities of notation. Some songs have traditional time signatures, others have only a 3 or 4 at the beginning to indicate a more swinging or walking rhythm. The absence of bar lines leaves the singer free to determine the musical phrasing according to the rhythm of the words and their sense. Commas indicate a slight pause, or point of rest.

*Jennifer Aulie*

References:

Knierim, Julius. *Songs in the Mood of the Fifth 'Quintenlieder'.*
ISBN 0 945803 14 1 (Rudolf Steiner College Press, California)

Steiner, Rudolf. *The Study of Man.*
ISBN 9781855841871 (Rudolf Steiner Press, England)

Steiner, Rudolf. *The Inner Nature of Music and the Experience of Tone.*
ISBN 9780880100748 (Steiner Books, USA)

M. Meyerkort                                               N. Foster

In the Ad - vent gar - den,

dark the night be - low,

Earth is wait - ing, wait - ing, wait - ing,

for the stars to glow.

### At the Lighting of the Advent Wreath

1. Winter is dark,
   Yet each tiny spark
   Brightens the way
   To Christmas Day.

2. Shine little light
   And show us the way
   To the bright light
   Of Christmas Day.

   *H. St. John*

17

From Germany                                                    J. Aulie

From heav-en's arch  so   high, __   A  lit-tle  light

draws   nigh. __   Stops  to  hear,   stands  quite  near,

Won - ders  what     is    happ' - ning  here.

2. The mother with her baby
   Calls the light in gaily:
   Come in here,
   Come in here,
   Light us with your radiance clear.

3. And shining ever clearer,
   The light comes softly nearer,
   In the night,
   Shines so bright,
   That the child may take delight.

4. Then all the lights divine,
   They bring their golden shine,
   And they bow,
   Deep and low,
   Bringing him their heavenly glow.

**Suggested directions:** *1st verse: a circle of children walks around while 2 to 6 children sit on chairs in the centre, and a further 2 to 6 children each hold a small candle and walk around outside the circle.*
*2nd verse: everybody stands still and the circle children and chair children make a beckoning gesture.*
*3rd verse: the circle children raise their arms: outside children enter and each gives her/his candle to one of the chair children and then joins the circle.*
*4th verse: the circle children cup their hands, advance to the centre and place their imaginary lights in the lap of the chair children.*

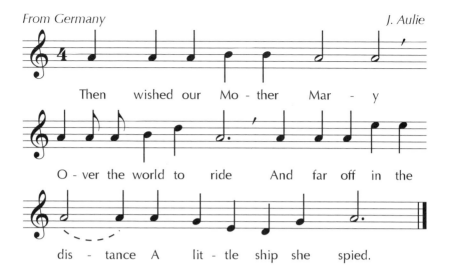

From Germany                                                    J. Aulie

Then     wished our   Mo - ther   Mar - y

O - ver the world to     ride     And   far   off   in   the

dis - tance A   lit - tle   ship   she   spied.

2.  Oh little ship, I pray thee,
    Come take me from this strand,
    Take me and bear me with thee
    To heaven's golden land.

3.  And when our Mother Mary
    Went forth a-journeying,
    The bells of all the world
    Began to sing and ring.

4.  They rang, they rang so brightly,
    They rang so bright and clear,
    They rang our Mother Mary
    Into the heavenly sphere.

**Suggested directions:** *1st verse: a circle of children, each with a little bell on a thread around their neck, walks around while 2 to 8 children, without a bell, walk outside the circle.*
*2nd verse: everybody stands still. Each child outside the circle softly knocks on the shoulder of a child of her/his choice, whereupon arms are raised and the outside children enter the circle and stand in the centre.*
*3rd verse: circle children gently rock from left to right and right to left without raising their feet.*
*4th verse: circle children walk around ringing their bells.*

1. Kind old man, St. Nicholas dear,
   Come to our house this year.
   Here's some straw and here's some hay
   For your little donkey grey.

2. Pray put something in my shoe,
   I've been good the whole year through,
   Kind old man, St. Nicholas dear,
   Come to our house this year.

*From Germany*

1. Upon his snow white steed
   With wind and lightning speed
   St. Nicholas leaves the sky
   And comes a riding by.

2. The little hare hops nigh
   And lifts his nose up high.
   The stag, with pointing horn,
   Jumps over bush and thorn.

3. And all creatures dear
   Are drawing quickly near.
   Before St. Nicholas bow,
   Their little heads so low.

4. And we will learn a tune,
   Of sun and star and moon,
   And sing our happy lay,
   Sing on St. Nicholas' day.

*From Germany*

Lyre:

From the sun down path of star - light
Soft-ly, soft-ly Mar - y treads, Weav - ing
for her Child a gar - ment Pur-est gold and
sil - ver threads. See now Mar - y

step - ping gent - ly    Watched by star - ry

choir so bright,    With her snow white

hand pre - par - ing    What de - scends on Christ - mas

Night.

2. Mary asks the sun to weave her
   For her Child a robe of light,
   Begs the moon then to bequeath her
   Peace for Him and pure delight.
   All the stars she gathers singing,
   To her coach she makes them fast,
   And while heav'n with joy is ringing
   Down she comes to earth at last.

3. *Repeat verse 1 to* 𝄐 .

23

G. Hayn                                                    P. Patterson

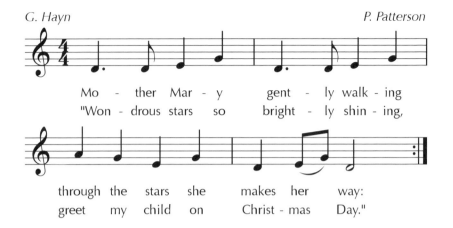

Mo - ther Mar - y      gent - ly walk - ing
"Won - drous stars   so   bright - ly shin - ing,

through the   stars   she   makes her   way:
greet    my   child   on   Christ - mas   Day."

2.  Wondrous stars, they see her coming,
        bow their heads and bid her stay:
    "Take from us a crown of starlight
        for your child on Christmas Day!"

3.  Mother Mary, gently walking,
        to the sun she makes her way:
    "Golden Sun, so brightly shining,
        greet my child on Christmas Day!"

4.  Golden sun, he sees her coming,
        bows his head and bids her stay:
    "Take from me a golden sunbeam
        for your child on Christmas Day!"

5.  Mother Mary, gently walking,
        to the moon she makes her way:
    "Silver Moon, so brightly shining
        greet my child on Christmas Day!"

*Continued...*

6. Silver moon, she sees her coming
    bows her head and bids her stay:
   "Take from me a silver girdle
    for your child on Christmas Day!"

7. Mother Mary, gently walking,
    down to earth she makes her way,
   Bearing gifts of heavenly splendour
    for her child on Christmas Day!"

8. Loving children see her coming,
    bow their heads and bid her stay:
   "Take our love, Oh, Mother Mary
    for your child on Christmas Day!"

1. The time draws near
   When greatest light
   In all the year
   Shines in the night.

2. The Child is born
   And by His Birth
   A rosy dawn
   Spreads o'er the earth.

3. Oh star so bright
   That shines in the night,
   Lead us to find
   The Son of Mankind.

4. Oh, see where He lies
   Before wond'ring eyes,
   Lowly His bed
   But crowned His head.

*H. St. John*

Softly, softly, through the darkness
   Snow is falling.
Sharply, sharply, in the meadows
   Lambs are calling.
Coldly, coldly, all around me
   Winds are blowing.
Brightly, brightly, up above me
   Stars are glowing.

*B. E. Milner.*

M. Meyerkort                                                                    N. Foster

In the Christ - mas gar - den,

where we sing - ing go,

Life is glow - ing, flow - ing, glow - ing,

red the ros - es grow.

A-swinging, a-ringing,
The bells at Christmas say:
A merry Christmas to you all
And happiness for great and small,
With joy we sing and plenty bring,
This happy Christmas Day.


Ring, ring, ring the bells,
Ring them loud and clear,
To tell the children everywhere
That Christmas time is here.


1. A wondrous sound steals through the night
   Like silver bells from distant height,
   Like voices filled with joy and mirth,
   Like stars alighting on the earth.

2. We wrap the earth in a silken gown,
   In glittering jewels from heaven's crown,
   In silent shoes that soundless go,
   Just as the Christ Child bade us do.

3. On Joseph's broad brimmed hat the snow
   Drifts down so gentle and so calm.
   While underneath the fir tree bough
   The little Child lies soft and warm.

4. He sleeps beneath the roof of green
   Nor feels the winter wind so wild,
   And all the forest watching keen
   Doth guard and keep the heavenly Child.

*From Germany*

From Germany                                                    P. Patterson

When Je - sus Christ our Lord was born It
Mar - y saw on her way a tree With

was so cold, _____ And
figs of gold: _____ "Oh

Mar - y leave the figs to grow, We

have a long way still to go, And

night draws near." _____

2. When Mary came unto the town
   She went her way,
   And knocked at a farmer's house and said:
   "Let us in I pray.
   'Tis for the little child I plead,
   Then be to us a friend indeed,
   The night is cold."

*Continued...*

3. The farmer kindly said: "Oh friends
   No room is free,
   But in this little stable here
   You may surely be.
   It will be dark and cold the night,
   So take with you this candle light,
   Good night to you."

4. And when the man awoke it was
   The midnight hour:
   "Wake up my wife, and take some wood
   To light a fire.
   I wonder how these poor friends are.
   They will be cold they walked so far
   And must get warm."

5. When Mary saw the farmer come
   And light the wood,
   She put the manger closer still –
   Oh that is good.
   A little kettle Joseph took
   And hung it on a rusty hook.
   The kettle boils.

6. The old man found a chip and carved
   A little spoon,
   Which then like crystal, diamond and
   Ivory shone.
   And Mary rocked her little son
   And everything he looked upon
   Was filled with light.

H. Hahn                                          A. Künstler

Hush - a - bye,   hush - a - bye,   ho - ly   night,

an - gels have    brought   the    Child   of   Light:

All    man - kind   shall   gent - ly   bear   Him,

all    the    beasts   shall   nes - tle   near   Him,

all    the    flow - ers   shall   a - dore   Him,

all    the    stones   shall   kneel   be - fore   Him,

all __ the    world   shall   wor - ship   Him,

*Continued...*

30

*D.C. al fine*

Cher - u - bim and Ser - a - phim.

*From Germany*                    *E. Pracht*

See deep in the moun - tains where the

wind blows wild there sits Ho - ly

Ma - ry and crad - les her child. She

rocks the crad - le with hands so white, she

needs but a touch for the babe so light.

M. Winship
M. Winship

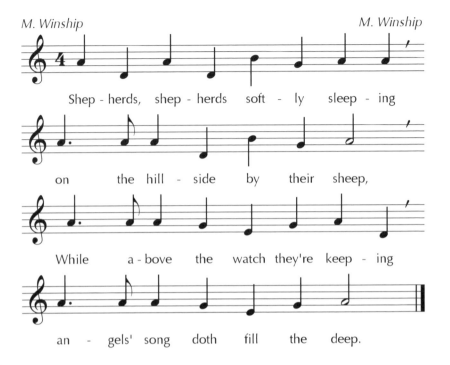

Shep - herds, shep - herds soft - ly sleep - ing
on the hill - side by their sheep,
While a - bove the watch they're keep - ing
an - gels' song doth fill the deep.

1. Mary rocks her Baby,
   Joseph holds a light,
   Ox and ass are standing
   In the stable bright.

2. Shepherds in the doorway
   Come to greet the Child,
   Now they kneel before Him
   And his mother mild.

3. One holds out a lambkin
   Soft and white as snow,
   All shall give their presents
   Ere they homeward go.

*H. St. John.*

32

Shepherds gather wood and briar,
Build and stack the evening fire.

Spot and Rover!  Come, and heel!
It's time to eat your evening meal.

On cheese and bread the shepherds sup
And drink clear water from a cup.

Gather moss to build your bed,
Make it smooth to rest your head.

Above the mountain shines the moon,
So shepherds sing your evening tune.

Cloaks are long and cloaks are warm,
Protecting you from frost and storm.

Spot and Rover!  Watch the sheep,
Shepherds need to go to sleep.

*M. Meyerkort*


See, the shepherds go to sleep
On the hillside by their sheep.
In the quiet, starry air
Angel song is everywhere.

M. Wilson                                                    M. Wilson

We are shep - herds and we sing of

lots of jol-ly things. We can dance and we can

shout, We can wave our caps a - bout. The

stars shine a - bove us, the snow shines be - low And

we are so hap - py in this wond - rous glow.

1.  Shepherds near and far,
    Behold on high a star.
    The angels fill the sky with light
    And sing that Christ is born this night.

2.  Rise and welcome day,
    We will no longer stay.
    And so we gather gifts to take:
    Some milk, some wool, some meal to bake.

3.  Then sing fa-rol-da-dee.
    The child we go to see!
    The star doth lead us on our way
    And so we shall not go astray.

4.  Lulla-lullaby,
    Behold where he doth lie!
    Now quiet shepherds one and all,
    There lies the child within the stall.

5.  Oh-Oh-Oh,
    We shepherds all bow low!
    We've come to you a gift to bring
    And now we will your praises sing.

6.  All people good and true,
    The light we bring to you!
    The light of Christmas shining bright
    We'll bear and love with all our might.

*P. Wehrle*

1. I, said the donkey, all shaggy and brown,
   I carried his Mother to Bethlehem town.
   I, said the donkey, all shaggy and brown.

2. I, said the ox, all white and red,
   I gave him some hay to pillow his head.
   I, said the ox, all white and red.

3. I, said the lambkin, as white as snow,
   I gave him some wool to cover his toe.
   I, said the lambkin, as white as snow.

4. I, said the spider, swinging down to the floor,
   I wove a web to make him a door.
   I, said the spider, swinging down to the floor.

5. I, said the robin, all red aglow,
   I fanned the fire to melt the snow.
   I, said the robin, all red aglow.

6. I, said the mouse, and poked out his head,
   I brought some corn to bake his bread.
   I, said the mouse, and poked out his head.

7. I, said the dove, on the rafter high,
   I lulled him to sleep so he would not cry.
   I, said the dove, on the rafter high.

## AT THE MANGER

*Cobbler:*    Hammer, hammer, Cobbler,
Tick-a-tack-too.
Lo, the Child will walk the earth,
So work a goodly shoe.

*Fisherman:*    Draw your nets, Oh Fisherman,
From the water's flow.
Take the little silver fish
To the manger low.

*Tailor:*    Thread your needle, Tailor,
Swiftly sew away,
Swiftly, deftly sew a coat,
The Child is born today.

*Blacksmith:*    Blow the fire, Blacksmith,
Heat the iron red.
Hammer ploughshares for the Child
To plough the earth for bread.

*M. Meyerkort*

To Beth' - lem I would go, _____ to

Je - sus he must know: __ at home I have a

black - cock so trim, a cuck - oo both brown and

slim, these will I give to Him.

Black - cock will make Him gay,

ne - ver will fly a - way, lit - tle cuck - oo

perch - ing near his head call - ing sweet - ly

sure to make him glad. _____ Coo - coo, coo-coo, coo-

*Continued...*

coo, _____ coo - coo, coo - coo, coo - coo.

Hail    to    Thee,    Ho - ly    Je - su.

1. Get up, little horsey,
   Go to Bethlehem;
   Tomorrow there is a feast day,
   Next day feast again!

2. Get up, little horsey,
   To the fair in town;
   Do not stumble, horsey,
   Or I'll tumble down!

3. Get up, little horsey,
   To Bethlehem go straight;
   Hurry, hurry, hurry,
   Or we'll be too late!

4. Get up, little horsey,
   To Bethlehem with you;
   There we'll see the mother
   And the baby, too.

*From Spain*

1. Come!  Let us go
   Through frost and snow
   To Bethlehem,
   Oh, all good men.

2. The trees bend low
   Their caps of snow,
   "We give a twig,
   We give a cone,
   To warm the little
      Baby's home."

3. "Oh, hark I heard
   A robin bird,
   What does he say
   This winter day?"

4. *Robin:*   I'll sing at dawn
             On Christmas Morn,
             So I'll come too,
             Along with you.

5. The shepherds sleep
   Among their sheep,
   An angel bright
   Comes in the night.

6. Awake, good men!
   To Bethlehem,
   The Child lies there
   In stable bare.

7. *Chorus:*   Ah!  Here we are
              By light of star,
              In Bethlehem,
              Oh, all good men.

*H. St. John*

M. Bucknall

N. Foster

J. Knierim                                                    J. Knierim

Swing - ing bells are ring - ing.

Hap - py child-ren are sing - ing:

Who is com - ing from a - far?

Kings of O - ri - ent we are.

Mel - chior, Cas-par, Bal-tha-sar fol-low-ing the

shin - ing star to the Child of

In - no - cence of - fer gold,

myrrh and frank - in - cense. _____

*Continued...*

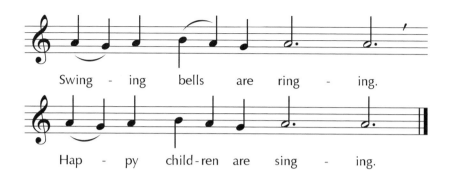

Swing - ing bells are ring - ing.

Hap - py child-ren are sing - ing.

Snowflakes so light,
Snowflakes so bright,
Cover the earth
And make it white.

*I. Tupaj*

Snowflakes falling soft and light,
Snowflakes falling in the night,
Soft and light, pure and white,
When the sun shines out so bright,
All the earth is dressed in white,
All the earth is dressed in white.

1. Kings came riding,
   One, two, three,
   Over the desert
   And over the sea.

2. One on a horse
   With a saddle of gold:
   The children came running,
   To behold.

3. One in a ship
   With a silver mast:
   The fishermen wondered
   As he went past.

4. One came walking
   Over the sand,
   With a casket of treasure
   In his hand.

5. All the people said:
   Where go they?
   But the kings went forward
   All through the day.

6. Night came on
   As those kings went by.
   They shone like the gleaming
   Stars in the sky.

M. Meyerkort

N. Foster

In the win - ter gar - den,

through the fall - ing snow,

Stars are gleam - ing, stream - ing, gleam - ing,

down to earth be - low.

2.  In the winter garden seeds lie warm below,
    Flowers are waiting, waiting, waiting for the spring to blow.

M. Meyerkort

N. Foster

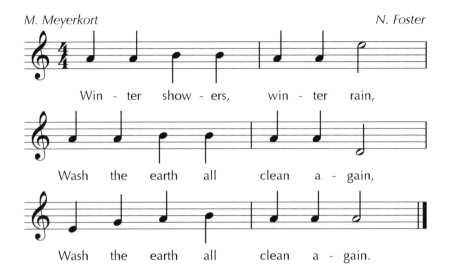

Win - ter show - ers, win - ter rain,

Wash the earth all clean a - gain,

Wash the earth all clean a - gain.

From Germany

Traditional German

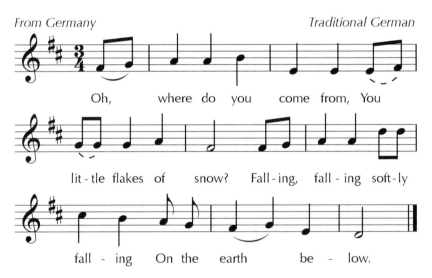

Oh, where do you come from, You

lit - tle flakes of snow? Fall - ing, fall - ing soft - ly

fall - ing On the earth be - low.

2. On the trees and on the bushes,
   On the mountains afar,
   Tell me snowflakes do you come from
   Where the angels are?

C. Comeras

On the wind of Jan - u - a - ry

down ____ flits the snow. _____

Trav - el - ling from the froz - en north, ___

cold as it can blow. _____

While we are sleeping through the night,
Snowflakes are falling soft and white.
Floating down with never a sound,
Silently covering all the ground.
Robin comes with his scarlet breast
Calling sweetly, "Wake and see."
We all get up and quickly dress,
Out to the garden rush with glee.
With sparkling eyes and cheeks a-glow
We romp and shout, "Hooray for snow."

*H. Henley*

*N. Foster*

Come, lit - tle snow - flakes, dance through the air, _____ Mak-ing the world ____ so pure and fair, _____ Light and bright, ____ spark - ling white, ____ Soft as the wings of the dove in flight. _____

Whenever a snowflake leaves the sky,
It turns and turns to say goodbye.
"Goodbye, dear cloud, so cool and grey."
Then lightly travels on its way.

And when a snowflake finds a tree
"Good day," it says, "good day to thee.
Thou art so bare and lonely here
I'll call my friends to settle near."

H. Henley                                                    N. Foster

The    snow    fell    soft - ly    in    the

night,    All    the    world    was    glist' - ning

white.    The    an - gels    from    the    stars    looked

down    On    Mo - ther    Earth's    new    shin - ing

gown.    The    moon - beams    danced    down

si - lent - ly,    And    kissed    each

spark - ling    branch    and    tree.

*J. Marcus*                               *J. Marcus*

See    the   Snow    King    and    his   Queen

Fly    in     the    sky     so      high. ____

Shak - ing   their    snow     flakes     as     they go, ____

Fall    -    ing,   fall    -    ing,     down    be - low.

2.    Where is our snow child, where is she?
       Hiding around the tree.
       Swirling, twirling round they go,
       Dancing, dancing in the snow.

1.    Go, Jack, go, Jill, and fetch your sled,
       It's snowy winter weather;
       Come, Jack, come, Jill, and climb the hill,
       We'll all slide down together.

2.    Go, Jack, go, Jill, climb up again,
       And bring your little brother;
       Come, Jack, come, Jill, we'll take a trip,
       And then we'll take another.

*C. Crane*

Roll the snow over and over.
Roll the snow over the ground.
Pat it and shape it
Making a snowball round.
Two balls we take for a body,
One for the snowman's hand,
Top with a hat worn and shabby,
Tie on a scarf, winter red.
Roll the snow over and over.
Roll the snow over the ground.
Making a smiling old snowman
Is the jolliest fun we have found.



We made a man all by ourselves,
We made him jolly fat,
We stuffed a pipe into his face,
And on his head a hat.
We made him stand upon one leg,
That so he might not walk.
We made his mouth without a tongue,
That so he might not talk.
We left him grinning on the lawn,
That we to bed might go:
But in the night he ran away –
Leaving a heap of snow!

Little light snowflakes
Whirl around.
Little light snowflakes
Fall to the ground.
Fall on the tree
And fall on me;
Make the earth white,
Make the earth bright.

*I. Tupaj*


Let's put on our mittens
And button up our coat.
Wrap a scarf snugly
Around our throat,
Pull on our boots,
Fasten the straps,
And tie on tightly
Our warm winter caps.

Then open the door . . .
. . . And out we go
Into the soft and feathery snow.


Mark your steps
With your feet
On the white snow.
Little holes,
Bigger holes,
Look, where you go.

G. Russell-Smith

C. Comeras

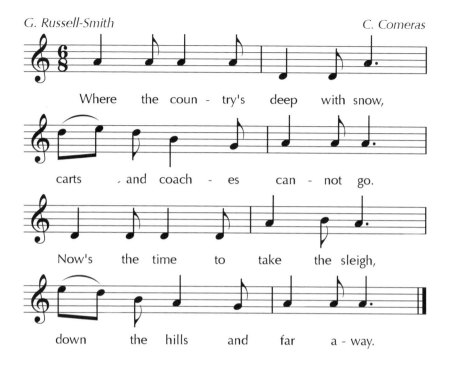

Where the coun - try's deep with snow,

carts and coach - es can - not go.

Now's the time to take the sleigh,

down the hills and far a - way.

2. Down the slipp'ry slope we slide
   Bumping swaying side to side.
   If you tumble now and then –
   Climb the hill and start again.


Let's go walking in the snow.
Walking, walking on tiptoe.
Lift your one foot way up high.
Then the other to keep it dry.
All around the yard we skip,
Watch your step, or you might slip.

M. Meyerkort  N. Foster

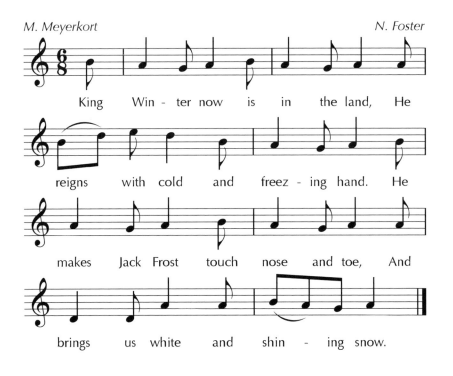

King Win - ter now is in the land, He
reigns with cold and freez - ing hand. He
makes Jack Frost touch nose and toe, And
brings us white and shin - ing snow.

I am a snowman, cold and white.
I stand so still through all the night.
With a carrot nose, and head held high,
And a lump of coal to make each eye.
I have a muffler made of red,
And a stovepipe hat upon my head.
The sun is coming out!  Oh, my!
I think that I am going to cry.
Yesterday, I was so plump and round.
Now, I'm just a river on the ground.

Make a ball of soft, white snow.
Pat, pat, pat, and watch it grow.
Big round snowballs, one, two, three.
Build a man of snow for me.
Sun comes out to warm the day.
Mr. Snowman melts away!


Jack Frost with freezing fingers fast and free
Flits o'er fields, makes fairies flee,
Fetch the fairy, fences fall,
Flowers fade, freeze them all.

M. Meyerkort


Jack Frost is very small,
I'm sure he is out today.
He nipped my nose
And pinched my toes
When I went out to play.


Who comes creeping in the night
When the moon is clear and bright?
Who paints tree leaves red and gold
When the autumn days turn cold?
Up the hill and down he goes
In and out the brown corn rows
Making music crackling sweet,
With his little frosty feet.
Jack Frost!

My igloo is round with a tiny low door.
It's made of cold ice and snow.
The inside is covered with blankets and fur,
So it's warm when the winter winds blow.


Five little Inuits by the igloo door,
One went out to feed the dogs, then there were four.
Four little Inuits rowing out to sea,
One jumped on an iceberg, then there were three.
Three little Inuits making fish stew,
One burned his finger, then there were two.
Two little Inuits hunting just for fun,
One chased a baby seal, then there was one.
One little Inuit all his work done,
Went home to supper, then there were none.


This is the way the snow comes down,
Softly, softly falling.
With a blanket pure and white,
Covering all the flowers from sight.
This is the way the snow comes down,
Softly, softly, falling.
This is the way the rain comes down,
Softly, softly falling.
Tapping, tapping as if to say,
"Wake up flowers, so bright and gay.'

Little dwarfs so short and strong
Heavy-footed march along;
Every head is straight and proud,
Every step is firm and loud.

Pick and hammer each must hold,
Deep in earth to mine the gold;
Ready over each one's back
Hangs a little empty sack.

When their hard day's work is done
Home again they march as one.
Full sacks make a heavy load
As they tramp along the road.

## GNOMES

With clang and clash in caverns cold
We gather glittering, gleaming gold.
With ding and dong in dark and deep
We search where silver secrets sleep.
With hey and ho in hundred homes
We mine the mountains' magic stones.

*M. de Havas*

## GNOMES

Crack, crack,
The rock we hack.
Quake, quake,
The mountains shake.
Bang, bang,
Our hammers clang.
In caverns old
We seek the gold.

1. Who is this I hear
   Deep down in the earth,
   Hacking and whacking
   The rocks and the stones?

2. We are the little men
   The dwarfs and the gnomes,
   We live in the caves,
   In the roots and the stones.

3. We want light like the stars,
   Yes, the stars in our homes.
   So we polish and shine
   The crystals and stones.


1. Oh, we hammer and bang
   And we make a great clang,
   As the iron we forge
   In the making of swords.

2. And we have the right tools
   For the cutting of jewels,
   That we polish so fine
   For a king's crown to shine.

   *B. Bushnell*


Knock, knock, the gnome
Hammers the stone,
Pick-a-tee-pick
Pick-a-tee-pack,
Glittering gold
Into my sack.

1. The little gnomes
   Are sitting on their crystal thrones.
   The red, blue, yellow precious stones
   Are all their homes.

2. We hammer and polish the gold crystal eyes,
   That sun, golden sun, can look in from the skies.

3. We hammer and polish the silvery eyes,
   That moon, silver moon, can look in from the skies.

4. We hammer and polish the diamond eyes,
   That stars, sparkling stars, can look in from the skies.

5. So all their homes
   Are red, blue, yellow precious stones.
   They're sitting on their crystal thrones,
   The little gnomes.

*M. Meyerkort*


Deep in the mountains are little homes,
Deep in the mountains live little gnomes.
Softly they sweep with a silver broom,
Stable and kitchen and barn and room.
When in the night a babe doth weep,
Gently they cradle him to sleep.
Hark in the stable moos a cow,
Little gnomes come to milk her now.

*From Germany*

1. Down the street the North Wind blows,
   Round the corner, there he goes.
   Hear him whistle, hear him shout,
   See umbrellas inside out.

2. Let him howl and let him blow,
   Still he brings the ice and snow.
   Let him bluster, let him boast,
   We'll go out to skate and coast.


1. Now that winter's come to stay
   All the trees are bare.
   Little birds must fly away
   To find their food elsewhere.

2. Little seeds lie hidden
   In the dark brown earth,
   Waiting until bidden
   To rise above the earth.

*S. Jarman*


1. Winter tells us little bulbs
   To tuck our heads in so,
   Then we will not need to shiver
   When the cold winds blow.

2. Spring will come with sun and showers
   Soon to raise our head.
   Then we'll grow and grow and grow,
   Right out of bed.

1. Cradled cosily, cradled deep,
   Wrapped in the warm earth baby seeds sleep.

2. Light we shed on you, light divine,
   Seeds in the darkness twinkle and shine.

3. Dream till the spring sun climbing the skies,
   Shines through the darkness and bids you arise.


Chip chop, chip chop,
The woodman with his chopper chops,
Chip chop, chip chop,
Stout and strong and proper chops.

On beeches, oaks and larches too
His hatchet brightly rings,
And while he chops so cheerily
As cheerily he sings.

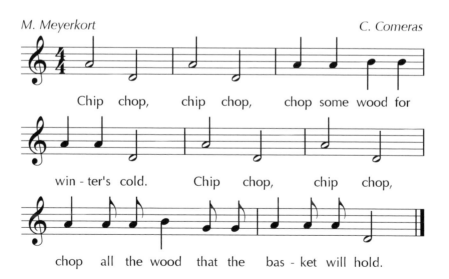

M. Meyerkort                                          C. Comeras

Chip chop, chip chop, chop some wood for
win - ter's cold. Chip chop, chip chop,
chop all the wood that the bas - ket will hold.

1. We are working, working hard,
   Chopping firewood in the yard.
   Hold the chopper, hold it tight,
   High we lift it, that is right.
   Chopping, chopping, chop, chop, chop,
   Merrily the pieces drop.

2. It's the finest game we know,
   Makes us warm from head to toe.
   Now a bundle we will tie,
   Put it in the shed to dry.
   Chopping, chopping, chop, chop, chop,
   Merrily the pieces drop.

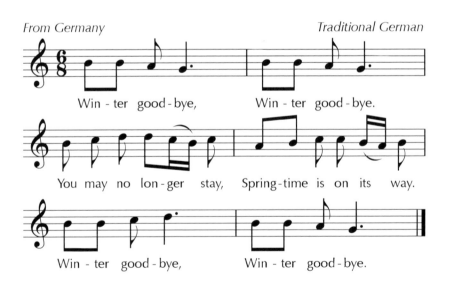

*From Germany*                                    *Traditional German*

Win - ter good - bye,     Win - ter good - bye.

You may no lon - ger stay,     Spring-time is on its way.

Win - ter good - bye,     Win - ter good - bye.

# Extracts from Nativity Plays

*These are not in sequence. Adapt to fit the aspect of the play.*

Mary:   Whence have you come, Snowflakes white,
      Flying to us in darkest night?

Snowflakes: From the cloud and from the star,
      From the lofty heavens far.
      An angel sang us lullabies,
      A star of silver bade us rise,
      And softly sailing through the night
      We make the earth a blanket white.

      1. When Mary wanders through the snow
        The cold doth bite, the wind doth blow,
        And all the creatures that there are
        In wonder follow the golden star.

      2. The snow-white stag with candle crown
        To greet the Child he bows him down,
        And Master Fox with bushy tail
        He sweeps a path across the vale.

Joseph:   The wind doth blow,
      And deep is the snow,
      Where shall we go?

Mary:   Oh do not fear,
      The angels I hear
      The stable is near.

Angels:   Little angels fly,
      Fly down from the sky,
      Spread your shining wing
      For the little King.

| | |
|---|---|
| *Shepherds:* | I saw a wonderful light, |
| | I heard the bells ring bright. |
| | Let us follow the star |
| | Though the way be far. |
| | |
| | A bottle of milk I'll take. |
| | And I some flour for a cake. |
| | And I soft wool a pillow to make. |
| | |
| *Shepherds:* | Open up the door, we pray. |
| | Shepherds we are from far away. |
| | |
| *Shepherds:* | We bend our knee, |
| | We bow our head, |
| | We lay our gifts |
| | Around his bed. |
| | |
| *Shepherds:* | I beg thee this milk to take. |
| | I've brought some flour for a cake. |
| | And I soft wool a pillow to make. |

*Each shepherd in turn to the Child:*

| | |
|---|---|
| | You and I, I and You |
| | We'll warm one another through and through. |
| | |
| *Joseph:* | We thank thee, Shepherds true. |
| | The starry light shall shine on you. |
| | |
| *Shepherds:* | Animal, you little brother, |
| | We will serve one another. |

*M. Meyerkort*

# Nativity Play for Young Children

*Children are in simple costumes, seated on chairs in a partial circle. In the centre are two chairs where Mary and Joseph will sit after they enter the 'stable.' The doorway to the stable is between the two innkeepers. The open side of the circle is the 'field' where the shepherds will stand or kneel. The number of characters can be adjusted to fit the number of children, e.g., more or fewer animals, or three angels.*
*Teacher leads Mary and Joseph around circle, while speaking:*

Once, long ago, it was the first Christmas, and Mary and Joseph were on a journey to Bethlehem. It was a long, cold journey, and Mary and Joseph were weary. When they came to Bethlehem there was no room for them in the inn. At last a kind-hearted innkeeper welcomed them into the warm stable where the animals slept.

*Innkeepers stand to light the way into the 'stable' with their lanterns. Teacher leads angels to stand behind Mary and Joseph. Angels hold their stars over Mary. Teacher continues speaking:*

In the middle of the night, when all was still, a Child was born to them, and they wrapped Him in swaddling clothes and laid Him in the manger.

*All sing the first verse of* The Friendly Beasts, *while making a rocking motion. Angels return to seats. Teacher leads the appropriate animals around the circle and into the 'stable' to give their gifts – e.g., donkey may bring a sack of meal; cow, a bundle of hay; sheep, a bundle of wool; dove, white feathers – while singing each appropriate verse of the song. After giving their gifts, each animal returns to seat.*

N. Foster                                                                    Traditional

On this cold mid - win - ter night was

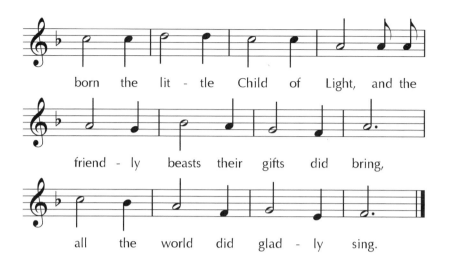

born the lit - tle Child of Light, and the

friend - ly beasts their gifts did bring,

all the world did glad - ly sing.

2. "I," said the donkey, all shaggy and brown,
   "I carried his mother up hill and down,
   I carried her safely to Bethlehem town,
   I," said the donkey, all shaggy and brown.

3. "I," said the cow, all white and red,
   "I gave him my manger for a bed,
   I gave him my hay to pillow his head,
   I," said the cow, all white and red.

4. "I," said the sheep with the curly horn,
   "I gave him my wool for a blanket warm,
   He wore my coat on Christmas morn,
   I," said the sheep with the curly horn.

5. "I," said the dove from the rafters high,
   "I cooed him to sleep so he would not cry,
   I cooed him to sleep, my mate and I,
   I," said the dove from the rafters high.

*Verses 2-5: R. Davis*

*Continued...*

*Teacher gives shepherds their crooks and leads them to kneel in the 'field,' while speaking:*

And in the field 'neath stars so bright
The shepherds watched their flocks by night, *(repeat).*

*All sing:* Shepherds, shepherds softly sleeping – see page 32.
*Teacher leads angels to shepherds, while speaking:*

Good tiding of great joy, the angel said,
For on this night in a manger bed
A Child of Light hath laid His head.
In Bethlehem He sleeps tonight
And brings to earth a wondrous light.

*Shepherds rise and prepare to follow angels.*
*Teacher continues speaking:*

And the shepherds said: "Let us go now unto Bethlehem, and find the Child of Light of whom the angel has spoken."

*Shepherds follow angels, led by the teacher, around the outside of circle to the 'stable,' singing:*

N. Foster                                                                    N. Foster

Let    us    go   now   to    Beth - le - hem,    And

find      the    Child      of      Light. _____

*Teacher continues speaking:*

And when they found the Child of Light they rejoiced and knelt before Him, and all helped to rock the Child.

*All make a rocking motion and sing a lullaby, e.g.,* Hush-a-bye, Hush-a-bye – see page *30.*
*Teacher continues speaking:*

And the shepherds returned home to tell the good news to the other shepherds.

*Shepherds return to their seats. You may repeat first verse* of The Friendly Beasts as an *ending, while the teacher puts out baskets to collect folded costumes.*

*Compiled by N. Foster*

# January Ring Game

**Song:** *On the wind of January – see page 47.*

Let's put on our mittens
And button up our coat
Wrap a scarf snugly
Around our throat.
Pull on our boots,
Fasten the straps,
And tie on tightly
Our warm winter caps.
Then open the door . . .
And out we'll go
Into the soft and feathery snow.

**Song:** *Come, little snowflakes – see page 48.*

Mark your steps
With your feet
On the white snow.
Little holes,
Bigger holes,
See where you go.

**Song:** *Where the country's deep with snow – see page 53.*

Now into the forest we'll go
Where the trees are covered with snow.
Sad is the forest, silence is king,
Not a movement: no bird can sing.

*Continued...*

All the flow'rs have fallen asleep,
Winter is long, winter is deep.
Frost is cruel gripping the bough,
Numbing hedgerows, piercing us thru'.
Magpie chatters, something is wrong,
"Where's summer now?" that is his song.
"Summer is gone, winter is here,"
Answers the frost, keen in his ear.

*Here could be other games sitting down: for example, "I can build a snowman," or, "Little white feathers filling the air," or, "This little kitten has lost his sweater."*

Here is the woodcutter sturdy and strong
With axe on his shoulder he strides along.

Chip chop, chip chop,
The woodman with his chopper chops.

Chip chop, chip chop,
To the ground the wood then drops.
On oak and beech and larch wood too
His hatchet brightly rings,
And while he chops so cheerily
He lifts his voice and sings.

**Song:** *Chip chop, chip chop, chop some wood – see page 61.*

Home we are walking as down sinks the sun.
Day's work is ended, tasks are all done.
The wood is all chopped for the fire so bright.
Now we'll be snug in our house tonight.

*Compiled by C. Comeras*

# St. Nicholas and the Star Children

Once St. Nicholas rode across the clouds from a country where the sun rises in the morning to a country where the sun says goodnight in the evening. Up in the heavens he met Mother Mary who was carrying the Christ Child in her arms and Mother Mary said to St. Nicholas: "Once again it is time that I take the Child down to earth for a while so that he can play with the children." When she had said this, many little stars came along from all sides of the heavens and asked whether they could go with them down to the earth.

"Yes," said Mother Mary, "but only if the moon will show you the way, for I cannot carry you all under my cloak."

When St. Nicholas heard this he rode off to the moon: "Good evening, dear Moon."

"Good evening, St. Nicholas."

"Dear Moon, will you please show these little stars the way to the earth."

"Yes, willingly, if the sun comes along too."

St. Nicholas rode to the sun. "Good morning, dear Sun."

"Good morning, St. Nicholas."

"Dear Sun, will you please help to take these little stars down to the earth?"

"What do they want to do there?"

"They want to play with the Child of Light and the children of the earth."

"That is how it should be," said the Sun.

And now the sun placed himself on one side of Mother Mary and the moon on her other side. The moon took the little stars in her lap, and the sun held the hand of the Child of Light who was sitting in his mother's arms. Thus they went together down to the earth, but St. Nicholas rode on in front of them. He rode so fast across the clouds that he arrived on the earth much earlier than the others. On earth he went from house to house and told everyone that the Child of Light would soon arrive, and he gave the children on the earth presents so that they could play with the Child of Light.

Then the Child of Light arrived on the earth accompanied by sun and moon. He jumped out of Mother Mary's arms and showed the little stars the path to the children on the earth, but when the little stars leapt out of the lap of the moon onto the earth, they had all become human children and played with the Child of Light and the other children on the earth. It was a happy game, for the children of the earth play more beautifully and happily when the Child of Light plays with them. Mother Mary looked on and smiled.

Many stars who had become children of the earth stayed with the human children; and when Mother Mary took the Child of Light back into the heavens, many children of the earth were allowed to go with her and the Child of Light, to live with the stars.

*U. de Haes*

# St. Nicholas

Once upon a time there lived far away in the east a pious man, the Bishop Nicholas. One day he heard that far in the west was a big town. In this town all the people had to suffer hunger, the children also. Then Bishop Nicholas called his servants who loved him and said to them: "Bring me the fruits of your gardens and the fruits of your fields that we can still the hunger of the children in that town."  Then the servants brought baskets full of apples and nuts, and on top lay honey cakes which the women had baked. And the men brought sacks of wheat. Bishop Nicholas had all these gifts taken onto a ship. It was a beautiful ship, quite white and the sails of the ship were as blue as the sky and as blue as the mantle of Bishop Nicholas. The wind blew into the sails and sped the ship along. And when the wind grew tired the servants took to the oars and rowed the ship westward. They had to sail for a longtime; for seven days and seven nights.

When they arrived in front of the big town it was evening. The roads were empty, but in the houses there burnt lights. Bishop Nicholas knocked at a window. The mother in the house thought a late wanderer had come and she asked her child to open the door. Nobody was outside. The child ran to the window. There was nobody outside the window either. But instead, there stood a basket filled with apples and nuts, red and yellow, and a honey cake lay on top. By the basket stood a sack which was bursting with golden wheat grains. All the people ate the gifts and once again became healthy and happy.

Today, St. Nicholas is in the heavens. Every year on his birthday he starts on his journey down to the earth. He asks for his white horse and journeys from star to star. There he meets Mother Mary, who gathers silver and golden threads for the shift of the Christ Child and says to him: "Dear St. Nicholas, please go again to the children and bring them your gifts. Tell them: Christmas is nigh and soon the Christ Child will come."

The earth is wide and great. Where St. Nicholas cannot go himself, he asks a good and helpful person to go to the children and take them apples and nuts, and tell the children of the coming of the Christ Child.

*From Germany*

# A Gift of Starlight

Once upon a time in a land far across the sea a baby king was born. The angels filled the sky and sang his story, shepherds and animals came and brought their gifts, cuckoos and doves and pigeons sang to him and wise men came to visit him. The baby king was happy to receive the gifts, but he wanted above all to give gifts to others. His mother knew this and she had a ship built for him, a white ship with curved bows and silken sails, and when the ship was ready it was laden with gifts. Then the mother took the baby king in her arms and stepped aboard.

The wind blew into the sails and the ship moved out over the sea. For many days and many nights it journeyed, following the pathway of sunbeams by day and of moonbeams by night. And when the baby king grew tired the waves rocked the ship and his mother sang to him.

One day the white ship sighted land faraway. But night was falling fast and there was no sunbeam pathway to follow to the shore. Thick clouds covered the sky and so there was no moonbeam pathway to follow.

High up in the night sky the radiant stars said: "We must shine through the clouds so that the ship can find its way." Then one star knew just what to do. He threw himself out of his starry home, down into the world below. He passed through the thick clouds and came to rest on top of a rocky headland by the sea.

And there he shone his starlight across the sea, and he lit up the water and the rocky coastline as brightly as if the morning star was shining. And his starlight pathway helped the white ship to make its way safely to the shore. And it landed, and the little king visited the people in that country.

"I saw three ships come sailing in on Christmas Day . . . . . in the morning."

S. Perrow

74

# The Lantern

Once there lived three peasants, Tom, Jim, and John. One day Tom heard people in the village say that the Christ Child had been born in Bethlehem and wherever Mary, his mother, had walked on her way to the stable white star-blossoms had sprung up. Tom hastened to tell his friends, Jim and John.

"Let us go there too," said Tom, and reached for his cap and coat.

"Ah," said Jim, "let us take something for the child. People say he is needy and poor."

"Yes, I'll take some fresh milk," said Tom.

"And I'll take a bag of meal so that his mother can cook him some porridge," said Jim.

John took a basket of eggs. He packed them in soft hay so that they would not break during the journey. The three peasants put on their thick coats and fur caps for it was bitterly cold. They took long strides in their longing to see the Christ Child.

When they had gone some way they saw a child who was sitting on a fallen tree trunk, crying.

"What is the matter?" asked the peasants.

"I have lost my way in the snow," said the child.

"I know you," said John, "you are Martin, the miller's boy. Come, Jim, take my lantern and light the way for us. I'll take Martin pick-a-back to the mill."

"I'm not coming," said Tom, "the miller lives a good half an hour from here and I am in a hurry to see the Christ Child."

"Then wait for us," said Jim and John, "we'll walk as quickly as we can and will be back soon."

But Tom had already leapt down the mountainside and was on his way. He came to a crossroads. Which was the way to Bethlehem? Tom did not know. He chose a road which led him further and further away from Bethlehem. And so he did not find the Christ Child.

Soon Jim and John came to the mill and Martin was glad to be home.

When Jim and John returned to the forest path it had grown dark. Suddenly Jim stopped in his tracks.

"Shshsh. There is a deer." The two peasants crept closer but the deer remained lying in the snow. It had hurt a leg when it had leapt through the frozen snow. John looked at the wound and Jim said:

"Come on now! We cannot stop again! I don't want to be the last to come to the Christ Child."

But John remained standing by the animal. Then Jim went on alone through the forest. He came out into the open country and a strong wind was blowing and his lantern went out. In the darkness Jim lost his way. So he went back to the forest and wandered about, calling for John. But John did not hear him. And so Jim was unable to find the Christ Child.

Meanwhile John ripped his hanky into strips and bandaged the deer's leg. Then he carried the animal into a sheltered hollow in the rocks.

"What can I give you to eat?" he wondered as he looked around. But everywhere was ice and snow. Then John remembered the hay in the egg basket. Carefully he took out the eggs and gave the hay to the deer. Straight away the animal began to eat. Now John had to carry the eggs without the hay and had to make sure they did not knock against each other.

When he came out of the forest John noticed that his lantern was almost burnt down, and a little way further on the candle light went out. The path was covered with drifting snow and he thought:

"If only I don't lose my way." He walked slowly and looked carefully around. Suddenly he saw a white star-blossom shining in the snow. It was a wonder how such a tender flower could blossom there. And when John looked up, to go on his way, he saw another star shining, and another and yet another, and whenever he took a step there again was a star-blossom. Then he knew this was the way that Mary had walked.

And so the blossoms showed him the way to the stable. Carefully John opened the door and squeezed through the crack. Light came towards him and he heard soft music such as he had never heard before. Mary noticed the peasant and beckoned him to come nearer. And when

John stood by the manger and saw the Babe he was filled with joy, and he said to himself:

'All I have are a few eggs, and yet I would like to give him so much more.' And so he asked Mary:

"What does the Christ Child wish for?" Mary smiled and answered:

"People have many wishes. The Christ Child has only one wish. He wants all human beings to love one another."

Then Mary looked at John's lantern and said: "Your lantern has burnt down." And she gave him a candle stump: "There, that is for your journey home." John thought to himself: "I shall not get far with such a little light," and yet he thanked Mary. He bowed in greeting before the manger and turned home. He sang as he went. When he had gone a long way over the mountain he saw that the little light was still burning. And then came a snowstorm. Snow and wind shook the lantern to and fro so that the glass panes rattled, but the light went on burning. At home his wife said:

"I was wondering whether your lantern would go out in that snowstorm and you would not be able to find your way." Then John told of the Christ Child and of Mary and the candle stump. And when they tried to blow the light out it flickered a little and went on burning. John and his wife laughed and hung the lantern on the wall above the corner bench.

Next morning the light in the lantern was still burning, and still it burnt the whole year through.

"It is always shining," said his wife, "to tell us of the Christ Child's wish.

*R. Hüttner*

# Robin Redbreast

The night Jesus was born in the stable was very cold. Joseph went out to search for wood because the fire he had kindled for Mary and the babe was in danger of going out. He was away longer than he intended because he could not find much wood. Mary became anxious that the fire might go out before his return. She was worried about the baby because she knew he must be cold. Suddenly some small brown birds which had been roosting outside the stable flew in and made a circle around the dying fire. They began to fan it with their wings and as the sparks appeared the remaining twigs and straws caught fire and burnt merrily. Mary threw a last handful of straw on to the glowing embers and the little brown birds hopped closer and beat the air with their wings ever more vigorously. In this way they kept the fire alight until Joseph returned with sticks and logs. But Mary saw that the birds had scorched their breasts in their efforts to save the fire, so she said to them: "Because of the love you have shown my child, from henceforth you brown birds shall always have fiery red breasts in memory of your deed of keeping the fire alight. People will always love you." And that is how the robins got their red breasts.

# The Nightingale and the Bird that Sang with the Angels

When the angels began to sing on Christmas night a little brown bird sang with them. He sang and sang for joy. He had never sung a note in all his life before, for he was a plain and dull little bird, a real sleepyhead especially at night, and all he had ever thought of was sleeping and eating.

When the angels had gone back into the heavens and the shepherds came down the hillside to the Christ Child the little bird remembered that he had been singing. He was so surprised that he fell from his perch on a tree into a bed of flowers growing beneath, which had blossomed out when the angels sang. "Fly, little bird, fly," the flowers whispered to him, "fly and follow the shepherds."

The little bird did so and thus it happened that he came to the stable and saw the Christ Child lying in the manger. How that little bird loved him! He was so happy that he longed to sing the angels' song again: "Glory to God in the highest and on earth peace to men of goodwill." He wanted to tell all the other birds that he, a plain brown bird, had seen the Christ Child. "I'll be the first one to tell them," he thought, as he flew back to his tree on the hillside. "How they will envy me and how important I shall be if I bring them the good news."

But while these proud thoughts about himself filled his breast, no song would come from his throat, only harsh noises came that disturbed the beauty of the Holy Night. He tried again and again but couldn't sing a note. This made him quite amazed and he even thought to himself: "This isn't fair, I was the first bird to see the Christ Child and really did sing gloriously with the angels. And now I cannot sing at all. The other birds will despise me as much as ever because I cannot sing." And while these thoughts filled his breast he remained unable to sing.

The next evening he flew again to the stable to watch the Christ Child. He found Mary was trying to hush the baby to sleep but the little one was restless, tossing about on his bed of hay, wide awake and almost crying. Straight away, with love filling his heart for the beautiful baby, the little bird flew to the manger, perched on the side and began to twitter a lullaby. Gently he repeated the words his mother had whispered to him and to his brothers and sisters in their nest, when they were baby birds. His mother, too, could not sing but she used to say softly to her babies over and over again: "Sleep, little one, sleep; hush-a-bye, hush-a-bye, sleep." And so the little brown bird whispered to the Christ Child these same words, thinking only of the restless baby, wanting to help him, pouring love out towards him. Soon the baby was asleep and the happy little bird flew out into the starlit night away to the hillside where the angels had sung. And now, thinking only of the sleeping Christ Child, he began telling of the happiness in his heart because the Christ Child was sleeping peacefully and Mother Mary had looked so radiant.

Suddenly the plain brown bird found he was singing for joy. All through the night he sang praises to the Christ Child and presently all the birds near Bethlehem awoke and listened in wonder to the music coming from the plain brown bird. For this was the hour when the bird we know as the nightingale first became a singer.

# The Little Fir Tree

On the night that Jesus was born three trees stood outside the stable. They were very excited about his coming and were talking together in eager whispers. The tall palm tree said rather proudly: "We must give him gifts; I know what I shall give him – a bunch of dates. He and his mother will love my sweet juicy dates. What are you two trees going to give him?"

The gnarled old olive tree replied: "My gift shall be some of my olives – Father Joseph will press them and give the oil that comes from them to Mother Mary. She will use it in many ways for her son – I am sure my gift of olives will be useful." Then both trees turned to the third, a very young fir tree and said:

"But what can you give as a present? You are so small, you have no fruit and even if you were big enough, you would only have hard cones which are no use to anyone. You haven't even any leaves, just sharp needles which would prick the baby if he touched you. Poor thing!  We don't know what you can give!"

The little fir tree was sad and would have liked to sink into the ground and hide itself. It murmured softly: "Yet I love him as much as you two big trees." But they didn't hear – they were wondering when Joseph would come out of the stable to pick their dates and olives.

Meanwhile it grew very cold. Jack Frost came by with his freezing breath. Everything he touched became coated in silver and white. He covered the three trees with ice and frost. They all looked beautiful, but the tiny fir tree sparkled in the starlight with its many needles each outlined with frost. Mary, looking out of the stable, was astonished at its beauty.

At dawn, Jesus awoke and looked out at the frosty world. The first thing he saw was the little fir tree sparkling and glittering with silvery frost. He clapped his tiny hands for joy and laughed with pleasure. Mary said: "Little Fir Tree, you have given my son a real gift. See how delighted he is at your beauty. Thank you, little Fir Tree!"

The palm and the olive bent down and whispered: "You have given him the best gift after all." And that is why we always have fir trees as our Christmas trees.

*From Germany*

# The Cloak

Once upon a time there lived a poor widow with her only son. He was a brave, adventurous boy who had always wanted to be a soldier. When he was old enough, his country had no need of him, so he decided to enlist in the service of a foreign prince – as was possible in those days – and at the New Year the widow's son was to leave his home and country to become a soldier of fortune.

His mother was fearful for him, but she knew he would never be content to settle down in their small village and follow the trade of his father, a weaver. So she had given him her blessing and planned to give him, as well, a fine warm cloak for Christmas. Though she was very poor she had spent as much, and more, time and money as she could afford. She had bought from the farmer his finest fleeces, shorn in the summer from the flock of sheep that grazed in the orchard at the back of her cottage, and spun from the wool firm soft threads. She had collected lichen, from the old trees in the orchard, stones in the church yard, and with it had dyed the two shades of golden brown. The darker made the warp, stretched on the best of her husband's two looms, the lighter made the weft, and though she was not so skilled as her husband had been, she was weaving a finer cloth than any she could have bought in the market at the nearby town: but it grew slowly on the loom for, less skilled in the weaver's craft, and with the housework to see to as well, she could not weave as quickly or as perfectly. She took so much time to fulfil the orders for cloth for customers that she had little time left for her own work. Only a few short weeks 'til Christmas, and the roll of finished cloth was not much larger than the roll of threads on the back of the loom, so she set about her work still harder, for after the cloth was finished, she had to cut and stitch the cloak.

The village where they lived was high on the moors and it was a cold winter that year. One night when she bad been working hard, her hands became so numb with cold that she had to stop. She laid down her shuttle, and the silence seemed more profound after the loud clippity clack of the loom. The rest of the village had gone to bed, no other light shone from the windows, all was quiet and still. After a day of storm, the gale had blown itself out, and the winter stars shone brightly. The poor woman could not work any more but neither could she rest. She stepped outside to stretch her legs and take a breath of air now that it was fine. She walked up the village street, the sound of her wooden clogs muffled by the mud, occasionally splashing through a puddle, until she passed beyond the last houses where the moors swept, round and bleak, against the sky.

By the gate in the low stone wall leading to a field, an old rusty plough lay abandoned. Above it, you could trace the constellation of the plough in the sky, so bright, there must be a frost on the way. The widow sighed as she remembered an old tale she had once heard. How Mary, the Mother of Christ, wandered from star to star taking golden threads from each to weave a garment for the Christ Child; how at this time of year, she was hurrying to finish it, ready for him to wear. The widow, too, was hurrying to finish a garment for her child, and as she turned back to go homeward she sighed again, for she thought to herself: "If I had star threads to weave into my son's cloak, they might indeed protect him from the dangers of the battlefield, from the cold winds of the north and the hot dust of the south. The cloak I am making is the best I can offer, but it is poor beside the armour and mantle I should like to give him, and poorer still beside the heavenly protection I pray may be his. If only I could weave star threads into my cloak!"

That night, she had a dream. Once more she was by the gate leading into the field, but instead of the field and moors beyond she saw a stairway leading to the sky. She climbed so high that the earth was far below and as she climbed, she saw at the top, standing on the moon's brow, Mary, with a smiling face and a crown of stars. Her outstretched hands were gathering long golden threads from the stars, her cloak was deep blue, so that the threads in front of it glittered. In her dream, the poor woman told Mary of the cloak she was making for her son; and begged for some strands of star gold for it. But Mary, 'though she smiled gently, spoke sternly to her: "You want star-threads from me – but what have you brought for me to weave into the garment for my son?" In her dream the widow wept and turned earthward again, for she had come empty handed. Though her face was wet with tears when she woke, she did not remember the dream nor know why she wept. All the next day though, it was as if she were waiting for something, expecting something.

Towards nightfall on a bitter cold day, a Sunday – the candles in church that morning had flickered in the draught of an icy wind – she heard a knock at the door. When she opened it an old man, ragged and frozen with despairing eyes hardly seen through the tangle of grey hair, stumbled against the doorpost. Hers was again the only lighted window in the village and the old beggar had been drawn towards it like a moth to a candle. Her son was out, and her first instinct was to shut the door and bolt it. In their small village any stranger was a foreigner and suspect, and this one looked wild, half crazed. But the voice in which he asked for food and shelter was weak, and she saw an echo of her own fear in the man's eyes. Stilling her own disquiet she went to her store-cupboard – not well filled – and found him some bread.

"I have no room in here, but we no longer own a cow, so you may shelter in the old cow-byre at the back." She gave him water, and the man went where she directed him quietly enough. But she was filled with anxiety until her son came home. He went to the cowshed and when he came back he reassured her; the old man was too frail to harm anyone and was sleeping like a child. She gave him some old sacks to take out to the byre and cover up the old man. In the morning, when she went out, to take a bowl of warm milk, the old man had gone. As she bent to pick up the sacks she saw a long fine golden thread, like a hair from the head of some princess, lying across them. She did not remember her dream, and went back to the house wondering how it could have come there. She took a fancy to weave it into her work, and did so, threading the strand in and out of the golden brown wool.

The cloth did not advance much during the next week. So many people were wanting their cloth for Christmas, that it was not until late in the evening of the next Sunday that she was able to work on her own cloth. She had just settled herself at her loom, when a neighbour's child knocked on the door, begging for a shovel-full of coals for their fire, which had gone out. Mother was not well, she said, there was no means of lighting another – would she come over? The widow was about to ask her to try next door, as she was too busy, when she saw the child's trembling lip. With a sigh, she got up, took the shovel and picking up some glowing coals from her own fire ran with them over the road to her neighbour's house. There she found a cold and cheerless room. Time passed quickly, but at last she was able to put the kettle on to boil, upon the fire which blazed at last, after much blowing and careful placing of logs, one by one. Before returning to her own house, she made her neighbour comfortable and saw to the baby. She returned to find her fire almost out and by the time she had saved it and banked it up for the night, it was too late to do much work – she could not afford to work too late too often. Regretfully she went over to her loom to loosen it until morning. Across the top of it lay another golden thread like the one she had found in the shed, fine as gossamer. Still she did not remember her dream, but again she took it into her head to weave the thread into her work.

The next week was stormy and windy again. It was fast approaching Christmas now, and her last bale of cloth had to be delivered to a merchant in the nearby market town a good few miles away. The washing, the baking and the finishing of the cloth had been so delayed by bad weather that she missed the carrier and had to walk to town with it herself, so that it might reach the merchant as she had promised.

The widow made the journey to the town safely, delivered the cloth, and, glad to be rid of the heaviest of her burden, set off home. She walked quickly, anxious, now that all the work for her customers was done, to get home and work steadily at her own cloth. If she could be home in good time, she might finish it that night; there was so little time left, so much to be done. As she neared home the short winter day was closing, the sky was dark with heavy cloud threatening snow. As she quickened her steps she heard a cry; some small animal in a trap, or a bird, or a kitten strayed from home, she thought as she checked her steps. She listened awhile but, hearing nothing, moved on. Again the sound came and this time she recognised it was human – the cry of a very young child. She searched the hedgerows in the gathering darkness. Just as she was telling herself that she was wasting time in foolishness, she came upon a little wicker basket almost under the hedge; in it was a very tiny child, not more than a few weeks old, half dead with cold. She lifted the child and hushed its feeble cry.

She was quite bewildered and could not think what to do. She had nothing at home to care for so young a child – her neighbour would not welcome another mouth to feed. The sense of waiting, of expectancy, which had so filled her for the last few weeks dissolved into impatience and anxieties. For one desperate moment she thought of putting the child back for some other passer-by to find. But the warmth of her arms stopped the child's crying and now that it was sleeping, she was reminded of her own son as a baby. It was a lonely road and getting late. She picked up the wicker basket and walked on, wrapping the baby in a fold of her cloak. As she walked she suddenly remembered that up on the hill some miles away was a convent. The good nuns had a hospital there, and an orphanage. She would take the baby there: it was a long way, but the best place for the little foundling. Before she reached her destination, snow was falling from the overcast sky, and it was dark. The kindly nun who answered her knocking exclaimed over her tale and took the child, assuring her that it would be well taken care of. Before she could leave, however, the abbess wished to see her and hear how she had found the child. The widow waited in a corridor near the chapel until the abbess could see her. In one of the walls was a small niche holding the statue of the Virgin and Child – and in front of the statue lay a third gold thread, exactly the same as the other two. For a moment the poor woman, who had forgotten her dream in the trouble and distress of her adventure, thought it must be an embroidery thread left behind by one of the nuns. But as she stood quietly winding the thread round her fingers, she remembered not only finding the other threads, but also her dream. She was tired now, and half asleep. As she looked at the little statue, it seemed to her as if she heard the same gentle voice say: "Now go home and finish your cloak. I have given you the star threads to weave into it because you gave me threads for my child's garment when you gave food and shelter to the old man, warmth and kindness to your neighbour, and shelter and safety to the foundling."

Wondering, she put the thread away carefully and, after telling the abbess how she had found the child, walked home. She was too exhausted to weave that night, but next day, as the snow-light filled the room through the especially big weaver's window, she wove in the third thread and her shuttle flew. The golden brown cloth was finished with the three golden threads so very closely intertwined they were invisible. It was Christmas Eve – by Christmas Day, she had it off the loom and soon it was fulled, and cut, and stitched, and her son wore it when he left on New Year's Day. His mother was sad to see him go, but she felt, as his cloak swirled around him, that the star threads would protect him from harm.

*E. Brooking*

# Shingebiss

In his lodge on the shores of Lake Huron lived little brown duck, Shingebiss. When the fierce North Wind swept down from the glittering land of Snow, four great logs for firewood had little brown duck, Shingebiss.

Brave and cheery was Shingebiss. No matter how the North Wind raged, he waddled out across the ice and found what food he needed. Pulling up the frozen rushes that grew in his little pond, he dived down through the holes they left and got his fish for supper. Then away to his lodge he went, dragging his string of fish behind him. By his blazing fire he cooked his fish for supper and made himself warm and cosy. At last the North Wind shrieked: "Woo-oo-oo! Who dares brave Big Chief North Wind? All other creatures fear him. Only brown duck, Shingebiss, treats Big Chief North Wind as if he were a squaw-breeze!"

So the North Wind sent cold, icy blasts, and he made high drifts of snow, until neither bird nor beast dared venture forth, save Shingebiss. Shingebiss still went out just as he had before and paid no heed to the weather. He got his fish every day, cooked his supper every night, and warmed himself by the fire. "Ah!" raged Big Chief North Wind, "little brown duck, Shingebiss, cares not for snow or ice! North Wind will freeze his holes, so he can get no food; then Big Chief will conquer him!" So the North Wind froze the holes where the little brown duck fished and heaped his pond with snow.

But, when Shingebiss found his holes closed so he could not reach the water, he did not even murmur. He just went cheerily on until he found another pond on which there was no snow. Then he pulled up the rushes there and made new holes for himself through which he could do his fishing.

"Brown Duck shall know who is Chief!" the North Wind howled in anger, and for days and days and days he followed the little brown duck. He froze up his holes in the ice and covered his ponds with snow.

But Shingebiss walked forth fearlessly, just as he had done before.

He always got a few fish before each hole was frozen and he still went cheerily home every night dragging his fish behind him.

"Woo-oo-oo! Woo-oo-oo!" The North Wind now roared in fury. "Big Chief will go to the lodge of little brown duck, Shingebiss. Big Chief will blow in his door, sit down by his side, and breathe icy breath until he freezes."

Now Shingebiss at that moment had just eaten his supper, and he was sitting cosily warming his little webbed feet by the blaze of his bright, burning fire.

Carefully, holding his breath, so Shingebiss should not hear him, quietly, very quietly, North Wind crept up to the lodge. But Shingebiss felt the icy cold come in through the cracks of the door.

"I know who is there," he thought. And he began to sing sturdily:

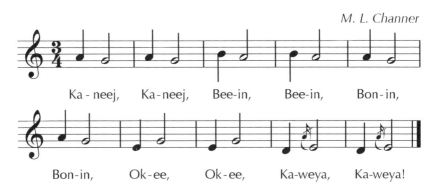

And the North Wind knew he was saying:

Continued...

Blow your worst, you can't freeze me, I fear you not, and so I'm free!

The North Wind was raging but he kept his voice to a whisper and he said: "Big Chief will freeze him!" So North Wind crept under the door, he slipped up behind little Shingebiss, and sat down by the fire. Now Shingebiss knew he was there, but he paid no heed at all. He kept on singing louder:

"Ka-neej, Ka-neej,
Bee-in, Bee-in."

"Big Chief will stay until he freezes," whistled the fierce North Wind, and he breathed his iciest breath. But, at that moment, Shingebiss leaned over and stirred his fire. A shower of sparks leaped up and the log glowed ruddy gold.

Then the North Wind's frosty hair began all at once to drip, his icy face started to drip, the tears ran down his cheeks, the mighty puff of his breath grew fainter and fainter and fainter. But Shingebiss still sat warming his little webbed feet by the blaze and he still continued to sing:

"North Wind, North Wind, fierce in feature,
You are still my fellow creature."

At length North Wind gave a shriek, "Big Chief is melting!" he cried. And he rushed headlong through the doorway and flung himself on a snow-bank. "Strange little brown duck, Shingebiss," he murmured weakly to himself. "Big Chief North Wind can't starve him, can't freeze him, can't make him afraid! Ugh! North Wind will let him alone. The Great Spirit is with him."

*A Chippewa Indian Tale*

# The Youth who went to the North-Wind,
## and demanded his Flour again

There was once upon a time an old woman who had a son. As she was very weak and ailing, she desired the youth to go up to the store-room and fetch some flour to make something for dinner; but when he was returning down the stairs, the North-Wind came rushing in, snatched away his flour and carried it off through the air. The youth returned to the store-room to fetch more, but when he was about to descend the stairs, the North-Wind came rushing in again and carried away his flour; and thus it happened to him a third time. At this the youth became very angry, and, as it seemed to him unreasonable that the North-Wind should act in such a manner, he resolved to go in search of him and demand his flour back.

He set off accordingly, but the way was long, and he went and went, until at length he came to the North-Wind. "Good day," said the youth, "and thank you for your kindness." – "Good day," answered the North-Wind. He was very rough of speech. "But what do you want?" added he. "Ah!" answered the youth, "I wish just to ask you if you will be so good as to let me have the flour again which you took from me on the stairs of the store-room; for we have but little, and if you are to act so and take the little bit we have, nothing will remain but starvation." – "I have no flour," answered the North-Wind; "but as you are so needy, you shall have a cloth, which will supply you with everything you could wish for, only by saying: 'Cloth, be spread, and be covered with all kinds of costly dishes.'"

With this the youth was well pleased, but as the way was so long that he could not easily reach home in one day, he went into a hostel on the road; and when those who were there were about to take their evening meal, the youth laid his cloth upon a table which stood in a corner, and said: "Cloth, be spread, and be covered with all kinds of costly dishes." Scarcely had he uttered the words, when the cloth did as it was ordered, and every one thought it a most wonderful thing, especially the host's wife. So when the night was far advanced, and every one was fast asleep, she took the youth's cloth, and laid one in its place that looked exactly like the one he had got from the North-Wind, but which could not furnish even dry bread.

When the youth awoke, he took his cloth and continued his journey; and that same day reached home. "Well," he said to his mother, "I have been to the North-Wind, and he is a gentlemanly person, for he gave me this cloth, which if I only say to it: 'Cloth, be spread, and be covered with all kinds of costly dishes,' I get all the food I could wish." – "Oh! Yes," replied the mother, "I dare say it is very true, though I would rather not believe it until I see it." The youth then in haste set out a table, laid the cloth on it and said: "Cloth, be spread, and be covered with all kinds of costly dishes." But the cloth would not furnish even so much as a piece of bread.

"Then there is nothing else to be done, but that I go again to the North-Wind," said the youth, and instantly he set off. Towards the afternoon he came to where the North-Wind dwelt. "Good evening," said the youth. "Good evening," answered the North-Wind. "I have come to get compensation for the flour you took from me," said the youth; "for the cloth you gave me is worth nothing." – "I have no flour," said the North-Wind, "but here is a goat I will give you, which makes pure gold ducats, if only you say: 'My goat, make money.'" This the youth thought was a fine thing to have; but as he was so far from home that he could not reach it that day, he took up his night's lodging at the hostel. Before he ordered anything, he made a trial of the goat, to see if what the North-Wind had said was true, and it happened just as he had said. But when the host saw this, he thought it was a most precious goat to have. So when the youth had fallen asleep, the host took another goat, which could not however make ducats, and exchanged it for the youth's goat.

The next morning the youth departed, and when he came home to his mother, he said: "The North-Wind is an excellent man after all; he has now given me a goat, which can make gold ducats. I need only say: 'My goat, make money,'" – "I know all about it," answered his mother, "and that it is all fudge; I will believe it when I see it." – "My goat, make money," said the youth, but not a penny did the goat make. So he went again to the North-Wind, and told him that his goat was of no use, and that he would have compensation for the flour. "Well, I have now nothing to give you," said the North-Wind, "save this old cudgel that stands in the corner; but its nature is such, that if you say: 'My cudgel, hit away!' it will continue striking until you say: 'My cudgel, be still.'"

As the way home was long, the youth went into the hostel again that night. And as he now guessed how matters stood with his cloth, and his goat, he lay down directly on the bench, and began to snore as if asleep. The host, who thought the cudgel was no doubt of some use, went in search of one that resembled it, and was going to put it in the place of the other, as he heard the youth snoring; but at the same moment that the man was about to seize it, the youth cried out, "My cudgel, hit away!" The cudgel then commenced beating away at the host, so that he jumped over benches and table, and cried and screamed for help. "Oh! For mercy's sake! Oh, for mercy's sake! Let the cudgel be quiet, or it will beat me to death. You shall have your cloth and goat again." When the youth thought his host had been sufficiently cudgelled, he said: "My cudgel, be still."

He then took the cloth and put it in his pocket, took the cudgel in his hand, tied a cord round the horns of the goat, and led him home. All this was good payment for the flour.

# Recommended Reading

*A is for Ox*, B. Sanders ISBN 9780679417118 Pantheon Books
*Failure to Connect*, J. Healy, Simon & Schuster
*Set Free Childhood*, M. Large ISBN 9781903458433 Hawthorn Press
*Rudolf Steiner*, R. Lissau ISBN 9781903458563 Hawthorn Press
*Lifeways*, G. Davy & B. Voors ISBN 9780950706245 Hawthorn Press
*The Spiritual Tasks of the Homemaker*, M. Schmidt-Brabant
    ISBN 9780904693843 Temple Lodge Publishing, England
*Education Towards Freedom* ISBN 9780863156519
    Floris Press, Edinburgh, Scotland
*Work and Play in Early Childhood*, F. Jaffke
    ISBN 9780863152276 Floris Books
*Festivals, Family and Food*, D. Carey & J. Large
    ISBN 9780950706238 Hawthron Press
*Festivals Together*, S. Fitzjohn, M. Weston & J. Large
    ISBN 9781869890469 Hawthorn Press
*Understanding Children's Drawings*, M. Strauss ISBN 9781855841994
    Rudolf Steiner Press, England
*The Wisdom of Fairytales*, R. Meyer ISBN 9780863152085 Floris Books
*A Guide to Child Health*, M. Glöckler & W. Goebel
    ISBN 9780863159671 Floris Books
*Education as Preventive Medicine – A Salutogenic Approach*,
    M Glöckler, Rudolf Steiner College Press, California, USA.
*Between Form and Freedom*, B Staley ISBN 9781903458891 Hawthorn Press
*Brothers and Sisters*, K. König, Floris Books
*The Challenge of the Will*, Margret Meyerkort & Rudi Lissau,
    Rudolf Steiner College Press
*The Oxford Nursery Songbook*,
    ISBN 9780193301931 Oxford University Press
*The Oxford Dictionary of Nursery Rhymes*
    ISBN 9780198600886 Oxford University Press

*Let us Form a Ring,*
  WECAN Waldorf Early Childhood Association of North America
*The Book of 1000 Poems* ISBN 9780001855083
  HarperCollins Children's Books
*English Fairy Tales,* J. Jacobs
*The Complete Grimm's Fairy Tales* ISBN 9780394709307 Random House
*Milly Molly Mandy Books,* J. Lankester Brisley, Puffin Books
*Seven-Year-Old Wonder Book,* I. Wyatt ISBN 9780863159435 Floris Books

# Acknowledgements

Further to the acknowledgement on page 3 of this book, the following is a list of permissions granted to reproduce previously published copyright material. Where it has not been possible to locate the original copyright holder, we tender our apologies to any owner whose rights may have been unwittingly infringed.

*Hush-a-bye,* by Alois Künstler, reproduced from Das Brünnlein singt und saget by kind permission of Verlag Freies Geistesleben, Stuttgart, Germany. *Where the Country's Deep with Snow,* the words by Geoffrey Russell-Smith reproduced with permission from Boosey & Hawkes Publishers Ltd, copyright 1968. *Softly, softly, through the darkness – titled Christmas Night –* by B.E. Milner, from The Book of 1000 Poems published by HarperCollins Publishers Ltd.

# Wynstones Press

**Wynstones Press** publishes and distributes a range of books, including many titles for children, parents and teachers.

Also available is a wide selection of postcards, folded cards and prints reproduced from original work by a variety of artists. Included amongst these are many works by David Newbatt, who illustrated the covers for this book.

**Wynstones Press** also distributes a selection of beautifully illustrated Advent Calendars, from publishers in Europe.

For further information please contact:

**Wynstones Press**
Ruskin Glass Centre
Wollaston Road
Stourbridge
West Midlands DY8 4HE.
England.

Telephone: +44 (0) 1384 399455
Email: info@wynstonespress.com
Website: wynstonespress.com